Birdies, Pars, & Bogies

Leadership Lessons from the Links

DAVID COTTRELL

ISBN: 0-9658788-0-5

Jacket design by Crabtree Design, Dallas
Book design by Defae Weaver
Edited by Alice Adams
Cover Photograph: Thorntree Country Club

1. Leadership   2. Success   3. Management

— *For Karen, Jennifer, Kimberly
and Michael*

TABLE OF CONTENTS

"Golf is deceptively simple and endlessly complicated. It satisfies the soul and frustrates the intellect. It is at the same time rewarding and maddening -- it is, without doubt, the greatest game ever invented."

- Arnold Palmer

INTRODUCTION

T his is the story of two friends, two caddies, and a golf game. The challenges experienced during this round are the same challenges millions of golfers face every day.

The game of golf is a great teacher of patience, etiquette, and emotional swings. This book concentrates on the lessons of leadership learned from this great game. You will read about forty-four different leadership principles experienced in the round of golf that is the focus of this book.

Enjoy the round as you learn *Leadership Lessons From The Links*.

BEFORE THE ROUND

I love to play golf. There is no better way to spend a beautiful April morning than here at the course. Last night's rain makes the grass even greener and the scent of the fresh flowers on the course more invigorating. The fairways and greens are freshly mowed. It is a great day to golf.

Today I am playing with my good friend and customer, Tod. He is already on the range warming up. My caddy, Tony, is studying the pin sheet. Tony is the master of the greens here at the club. He knows the hidden undulations on every green. He will save me some strokes today. Tod's caddy is Joe, a real nice guy that knows golf and also knows this course.

Before I hit the range, I need to stop at the pro shop to get a sleeve of black Titleist and check out the latest equipment. Man, has technology improved the game! I remember hitting persimmon then metal and now titanium; hitting steel then graphite and now bubbles; hitting blade then cavity and now oversize.

These changes in technology have made it possible for everyone to create customized clubs. They now have clubs and shafts that fit me and my game. The perfect clubs for my imperfect swing. I still buy new clubs every few months. I have a real problem in that area. My wife thinks I am a true "golfaholic".

I am looking forward to playing Tod today, but I am also preparing for next week's match play championship. In that tournament, there is a penalty for carrying more than 14 clubs. I had 16 clubs in my bag this morning so I left my 5 wood and 4th wedge in my trunk -- next to the five putters I have in there. I have all the clubs I need.

It's time to warm up and get ready. I used to stay at the office to the last minute and start my round without warming up. The first four holes were a disaster. I don't do that anymore. My new pre-round routine takes 20 minutes and makes a big difference! It includes stretch-ing, then hitting four solid shots with every other iron and then 5 good drives. After that, I putt for ten minutes to get the feel of the green and gain confidence before the round.

We just got called to the tee. Let's go play some golf!

LEADERSHIP LESSONS FROM BEFORE THE ROUND:

Successful leaders hire the best. Just as you choose the right equipment and right caddy to enhance your golf game, the most important activity of a leader is surrounding yourself with great followers who are also great leaders. More than 80% of our success is determined by the people we hire.

The effective leader continually evaluates his staff and ensures each is working at getting maximum productivity. If you have more people than you need, there is a penalty in lost profits. Leaders make sure they have the right people in the right place for their success, and eliminate the extra load created by unproductive employees.

Successful leaders use technology to improve their effectiveness within their organization. The ability to immediately communicate worldwide with clients and with employees in the field is a competitive advantage.

To stay at the top of their field, outstanding leaders keep themselves and their company on the leading edge of technology.

"The best executive is the one who has sense enough to pick good people to do what he wants done, and self restraint enough to keep from meddling with them while they do it."

— *Theodore Roosevelt*

TEEING IT UP

The walk from the putting green to the first tee is my time to get mentally prepared. I am ready for a good round and know the first shot sets the tone. Tod is up first and hits a two iron right down the middle.

Now it's my turn. The next group is at the tee watching and I am a little nervous. This is the toughest shot of the day. My ego is at stake. But, I am prepared for this shot and this round. Tony reminds me to stick with my pre-shot routine and hit it down the middle.

My pre-shot routine is systematic and helps my confidence:

- I visualize the ball in the middle of the fairway
- I believe in my swing
- I take my time
- I concentrate on hitting the ball squarely

My first shot on the course should be the same as my last shot on the range -- but it is not. This one counts and that makes a big difference.

I am ready. I enjoy the pressure. I step up to the tee, double check my alignment, and swing smooth and easy.

The shot is perfect.

LEADERSHIP LESSONS FROM TEEING IT UP:

Effective leaders take the time to mentally prepare for the task at hand. A few minutes of personal quiet time can set the stage for accomplishing the goals for the day.

Great leaders have a guiding vision, a vision of where you want to lead and a vision understood by your followers. To have a guiding vision, you must have crystal clear clarity in the end result (middle of fairway), have followers that believe in you (belief in your swing), have an appropriate timeframe for the result (take your time), and commit yourself and your followers to the end result (hit the ball).

"The game is played from the ground up."

— Ben Hogan

IN THE FAIRWAY

The first shot is down the middle, in the short grass. Right where I planned to be - 150 yards away - nice, smooth, easy 8 iron to the kidney shaped green. Not bad for the first shot of the day.

Tod's 2 iron left him 190 yards away and he came up short on his second shot. He gets a stroke here so I need to make sure I get my par.

Here is what I need to do:

- Move the pine chip behind the ball without touching the ball -- could create a wicked spin if not moved

- Visualize the ball clearing the trap and taking two hops to the hole stopping in the middle of the green

- I affirm: "I can do it"

- Take dead aim and strike it

Good swing! Good shot! Right over the trap, on the green, 30 feet away. I two putt for an easy par. Great start!

Tod makes bogey but he gets a stroke -- no blood.

LEADERSHIP LESSONS FROM THE FAIRWAY:

Effective leaders create a positive environment while keeping a positive attitude. Manage your attitude by continually looking for the best in your employees, eliminating things that could put a wicked spin on your mission, and look for the best in yourself. Be a champion at positive self talk that reinforces your ability -- I can, we will, I am prepared -- all contribute to your confidence in taking dead aim at your mission.

Leaders know how to enjoy the good times while preparing for the challenging times. Your success should be appreciated and enjoyed -- while you do what is necessary to ensure future success.

"The longer I live, the more I realize the impact of attitude on life."

— *Charles Swindoll*

IN THE ROUGH

My round is going pretty well. I bogied number two but did not play the hole that bad. My drive landed in a divot and I was not able to get on the green in regulation. Tod sunk a 8 ft. putt for par to go one up. If the hole had not gotten in the way, it would have gone ten feet past.

My drive here on number three was too good. It went through the fairway. I think it will be all right, though. I'll just have to wait until we get there to see.

Uh-oh, I didn't expect this. This rough is deep. The bermuda grass is strangling the ball and I can barely read Titleist. Seventy-five yards to the green, pin at back but no bunkers in front. My choices are to blast it out to the fairway with a sand wedge or punch a 7 iron towards the green. I have a flyer lie but I feel good about the punch shot and Tony agrees. No big risk hitting toward the green -- let's create something positive and get it on.

I get it out and it runs to the fringe.

I liked that shot! An easy chip from the fringe and tap it in for a par. Tod was all over the place. He took a double bogey and we are back to even.

LEADERSHIP LESSONS FROM THE ROUGH:

Outstanding leaders cope with the unexpected and create positive change. All businesses have unexpected changes that results in growth or grief. To create a positive change environment, successful leaders:

- Earn trust from their subordinates long before the change occurs
- Involve their people in developing the alternatives
- Commit totally to the change
- Press forward

Excellent leaders are long-term thinkers. They think beyond the immediate crisis to understand what is the best long term solution for their followers.

"Accept the challenges so that you may feel the exhilaration of victory."

— *George J. Patton*

LEADERSHIP MULLIGAN

The number one reason employees are unhappy at work is because they do not know what is expected.

ON THE GREEN

I took a bogey on number four, a par five. A fat six iron cost me a stroke. I really hate to bogey par fives. I will make that up on number 14, an easy par 5. Tod played conservatively and parred the hole to go back up.

Number five is one of my favorite holes. It's a 170 yard par three over a beautiful waterfall. I hit a perfect six iron. 18 feet away, uphill, slight break right to left. Tony was able to give me the read. He is the master at reading putts. I see a little left to right but I think his read is correct. The bentgrass is smooth as glass and the new no spike rule has really helped the green. I love this putt. I have been working hard at my short game because I read that it is 65% of the total game. If I don't putt and chip well, I don't score well. This putt is mine!

In the bottom -- that was a nice birdie. The putt broke exactly like Tony said. I putted six inches outside the right edge and it died right into the hole. That is one stroke Tony saved me today!

One over after five for a nine handicapper. Not bad! Tod makes a par and gets no strokes on this hole. We are now even and Mo is on my side.

LEADERSHIP LESSONS FROM ON THE GREEN:

The successful leader knows how to keep focused and concentrate on the critical success factors. Just as in golf where mastery of the short game is the stroke saver, there are a few vital functions within your business that deserve your constant focus and concentration. Be brilliant on those basics. If your employees do not understand what those critical success factors are and are not focused on improvement, your company will not grow.

Your value is eliminating all of the non essential activities and focusing on the vital, meaningful ones.

Leaders know that the 80/20 rule applies in their business just as it does on the golf course. Eighty percent of their improvement will come from 20% of their activities. Identifying the right 20% is the key to improvement.

Leaders listen to their employees and have the courage to act on their suggestions even though they may be different from their own.

The most effective leaders spend the majority of their time *listening* to their employees and their customers.

Effective listening skills are a basic requirement for effective leadership.

"Effective executives do one thing at a time, the most important thing, and they stay with it until it is done."

— *Peter Drucker*

My Opponent, My Customer

Today, I've got 3 more hours to be with my customer, Tod. I'm sure he doesn't want to talk business for 3 hours. I probably have about 5 two minute snipits to cover some issues. Now, when do I do it - probably best to wait until the turn when we are relaxed and in the groove. I can cover the opportunities then and summarize at the 19th hole. I know my points and will drop them at the right time. That is the right strategy for today.

LEADERSHIP LESSONS FROM MY OPPONENT, MY CUSTOMER:

Successful leaders make their meetings productive. There are five keys to conducting productive meetings:

- Have a good reason for the meeting. What is the purpose? How long are we investing in this meeting? What are we to accomplish?
- Always follow a published agenda
- Start and stop on time
- Deal with most important items first
- Summarize the results, agreed upon actions, responsible party for actions and when the actions are to be completed

Effective leaders set priorities. They know that the timing in pursuing an opportunity, is just as important as the opportunity itself. Set your priorities for what is important at that time and wait for the right timing on the rest of your list.

Effective leaders honor their employees and their customer's time. They know that the most valuable asset of their company and their customer is time.

The ability to communicate in a simple, clear manner to all levels of employees is a talent that must be learned and nurtured.

"There is no such thing as a self made man. You will reach your goals only with the help of others."

— *George Shinn*

LEADERSHIP MULLIGAN

Executives' Greatest Time Robbers:
- *Interruptions*
- *Being Disorganized*
- *Procrastinating*

A Snowman

This round is rolling along. I birdied number 6 for my first birdie-birdie this year. Tod bogied and now I am one up and hot.

Number 7 was friendly to me. A par three 200 yards -- my three iron was way short but hit a sprinkler head and rolled to within 10 yards of the green. Up and down for par. Tod parred and had no stroke so we tied that hole. I am still one up.

Number 8 was a easy 370 yard par 4. Three wood, nine iron two putt par - just the way it was drawn up. Tod took a double to go two down. Now, I smell blood.

Number 9 was a problem. My wheels came off completely. Okay, let's see. One off the tee, two in the water, three out, four in the trap, five in the trap, six on, and two putt. Yikes, a snowman, but nobody saw the flubbed shot in the trap. A seven sure looks better than an eight on the card - but I had an eight. Give me an 8. Tod took a par. He and Joe, his caddy, are high fiving -- you would think they won the Masters. I am still one hole up in the match.

I had a 40 on the front - Tod had a 42.

LEADERSHIP LESSONS FROM HAVING A SNOWMAN:

Effective leaders have integrity and earn their followers' trust. There is no reason in your business or personal life that outweighs the negative consequence of sacrificing your integrity. There are five principle elements of integrity in leadership:

- Keep your promises to your followers and everyone else
- Stand up and speak out for what you believe
- Always err on the side of fairness
- Live what you teach
- Do what you say you will do

Without integrity, you can't develop trust; without trust, you can't develop people; without people, you won't have followers; without followers, you can't be a leader.

○ **Outstanding leaders know that a charismatic personality will draw followers for a short period** -- only leaders with integrity will keep them through sustained trials.

○ **Followers demand honesty from their leaders.** Even with the ability to lead, vision to direct, and the greatest motivation techniques -- there are no followers without the leaders earning their trust.

"In golf, as in life, it's the follow through that makes the difference."

— *Anonymous*

ENJOYING THE ROUND

W e are at the turn. Glad to get that last hole out
of the way. I've hit some good shots so far and feel
pretty good about things. My customer, Tod, had a 42
and is ecstatic. He is a 21 handicap.

What a great day. Clear skies, no wind, and even with
my snowman I am still just 4 over par, a 40. This is not
bad at all for a 9 handicapper. I am doing what I want
to do and I am doing it pretty well. I love this game!

Leadership Lessons From Enjoying The Round:

○ **Successful leaders have a passion for leading.** Even though your days are filled with challenges, successful leaders enjoy their jobs and create environments in which employees can enjoy their jobs.

When your leadership position is in conflict with your values, then your passion for leading will leave and your stress will arrive. Keep your values in check with your actions.

○ **Leaders know that people will follow only those that have a desire to lead.** You cannot fake your desire to be the leader. Be true to yourself and your people.

"Golf, in my view, is the most rewarding of all games because it possesses a very definite value as a molder and developer of character."

——Bobby Jones

TREE PROBLEMS

Okay. We have our business behind us. Tod and I were able to agree on who needs to do what and we both feel good about our agreement.

Now, back to the match. Number 10 is a narrow 425 yard par 4. This is a tough fairway to hit and I faded my drive into the trees on the right. I'll just have to wait and see what lies ahead.

This is a problem! 170 yards out right behind the trunk of a live oak tree with low hanging limbs. They should have cut the branches -- carts can't even go under them. Well, what are my choices? If I get around the tree with a low screamer, I can get on the green. I could slice it around - maybe a 15% chance of getting on green. I can hook it around - maybe 20% chance. Or I can punch out about 60 yards, hit a wedge and try to get up and down. I'd better punch it out.

After my punch shot into the fairway, my 60 degree wedge puts the ball eight feet away and I par just as planned. Tod chips in for a par, to take his second hole in a row. He is unconscious this round. He better hope he doesn't wake up.

We are even again.

LEADERSHIP LESSONS FROM TREE PROBLEMS:

Successful leaders know how to solve problems. The leader needs a systematic process to solve each problem. Effective problem solving involves putting the problem on paper. Although you can't do that on the course, in business if you properly identify the problem -- in writing -- the problem is almost solved. What is the problem? What is the impact. What is the result if solved? Then analyze the alternatives, develop solutions and execute the plan.

A great leader recognizes a problem before it becomes an emergency and knows there is something he can do about it. Never leave a ball mark on the green – solve the problem now!

"The significant problems we face cannot be solved at the same level of thinking we were at when we created them."

— Albert Einstein

LEADERSHIP MULLIGAN

Always err on the side of fairness.

MISCLUBBED!

Number 11 ate my lunch. I topped my drive, sliced my second shot, and never recovered. A double bogey six on one of my favorite holes. Tod also double bogied but had a stroke and is now 1 up.

Number 12 is a 160 yard par 3. I feel good about getting back on track this hole.

I hit it solid but my ball flies the green. What happened? My 7 iron goes 160 yards. I hit it perfectly. How could it fly the green?

Oh no, I hit a 5 iron! Tony, I asked for a 7 iron. Why did you give me a 5? I hit the 5 you gave me and now I am 20 yards over the green and have to hustle for par, at best.

I recover with a nice chip but two putt for a bogey. Tony feels pretty bad but I should have noticed the loft before I hit. I made sure to let him know it was not his fault, it is my responsibility.

Tod's caddy, Joe, who has hardly said a word all day, is rubbing it in on Tony, telling him he can read the greens but can't read the number on the club. I thought Joe was a nice guy.

Tod parred the hole and goes two up.

LEADERSHIP LESSONS
FROM MISCLUBBED:

Successful leaders are excellent communicators. To communicate effectively, you must master the laws of communication:

- Keep It Simple
- Communicate With Crystal Clear Clarity
- Learn To Listen Effectively
- Check For Understanding
- Reward What You Want Accomplished

Successful leaders accept responsibility. The ultimate responsibility for the employees' actions rest with the leader. Blaming is counter- productive to your success. Accept the responsibility, create a system to ensure the failure does not reoccur and move on.

Leaders know that to be respected, you have to treat your employees with respect.

The universal wisdom of the golden rule is best demonstrated by its appearance in one form or another in every major religion in the world. It is the basis for long term success, "Do unto others as you would have them do unto you."

"Hold yourself responsible for a higher standard than anybody else expects of you. Never excuse yourself."
                                        - Henry Ward Beecher

212 Yards
Out Over Water

I did get back on track on number 13. An easy two putt par to get me going again. Tod is on a roll, parring his third of the last four. He does not need many strokes today. He is now 3 up with five to go.

Number 14 is my hole. 496 yard par 5 downhill I can reach in two if I get a good roll. I have the definite advantage on Tod with his 2 iron tee shot. He has no confidence in his driver.

I kill my drive. With a slight draw, it will be well down the hill and I should have a decision to make. After reaching the ball, I know I can get on this green in two and be putting for eagle. The only problem is carrying 212 yards over the water to the hole. I have a good lie. I am hitting my long irons solid. There is no wind to worry about. I can do it! Tony, give me my 3 iron and let's hit it on the green.

What a shot! 18 feet away. I can hear my imaginary gallery yelling "You're the Man!" I miss the eagle but tap in for birdie. Tod hits three 2 irons, 2 wedges, and 2 putts for a double.

I pick one back up, I am two down with four to go.

LEADERSHIP LESSONS FROM 212 YARDS OUT OVER WATER:

Successful leaders have courage to take risks as long as it is smart, calculated, and the reward is worth the risk. Leaders must have courage to:

- Give negative feedback to superiors
- Take risks when it is worth it
- Stay the course -- when timing is not right to change
- Know there might be other ways that are just as good or better

Leaders look beyond the obstacles keeping them from their goal and focus on doing what's necessary to clear those obstacles to their success.

Never take your eyes off your goals.

"The difference between amateurs and pros is amateurs look for the hazards and pros look for the landing area."
— ***Lee Trevino***

43

Leadership Mulligan

The opposite of courage is conformity.

Been Here, Done This

My eight iron on the par three 150 yard 15th hole came up short and my chip was also short. I two putted for a bogey. It is amazing how many times a birdie is followed by a bogey. Tod also bogied and he didn't get a stroke. No damage.

The wind picked up while we were on the 15th. The 150 yard 8 iron came up ten yards short when I hit into the breeze. I have a similar shot here on 16 and I don't want to be short and go into the front bunker. I am much better hitting a smooth 6 iron than I am hitting a perfect 7 iron. Based on my results on the last hole, I hit the 6. Good shot, back of the green, easy two putt par.

Tod did not think through the wind. He hit the exact same shot he hit on 15 and got the same result. Short of the green, he bogied again and had no stroke. He looked like a 21 handicapper on these last two holes.

Now I am only one down with two to go.

LEADERSHIP LESSONS FROM
BEEN HERE, DONE THIS:

○ **A successful leader understands their capabilities and the capabilities of their people.** They determine what is the right decision at that time and mentor their peers by drawing from their past experiences.

○ **A leader knows their areas of excellence and utilizes their time where they can do the most good.**

To help you make the best use of your time and your people:
- Work in your area of excellence, where you are the best 80% of the time
- Work where you are learning 15% of the time
- Work where you are weak 5% of the time

Allow your employees to supplement your areas of weakness.

"Failure is success if we learn from it."

- Malcolm Forbes

AFTER THE BIRDIE

The 17th is another birdie hole. 545 yards: I can't reach in two but it is a good 3 shot par 5.

After a good high draw, my drive lands 255 yards from the hole. The green is surrounded by water and I want to hit my third shot from 100 yards out. I hit a 155 yard eight iron and have a 100 yard pitching wedge left. My wedge leaves me 25 feet for my fourth birdie of the day.

Tod has to lay his third shot up and is on in four. His 60 foot par putt almost went in the hole and he taps in for his bogey. He gets a stroke so I have to make my birdie to win the hole.

Tony tells me to hit it straight at the hole. This is what I go with. The putt feels good, looks good and drops!

Not bad, 25 foot birdie putt in the dead center. What a putt! Played the hole perfectly. Way to go! Tony is pretty proud of that read. It broke left then right and then in the hole. He is the master!

I win the hole to even up the match with one to go.

Let's go play the next hole. I can't stand around celebrating. It is time to move on and make another birdie.

LEADERSHIP LESSONS FROM
AFTER THE BIRDIE

Successful leaders do not live in their past success.
They enjoy their success, learn from it, move on
and draw on the positive experience when needed.

Leaders do not procrastinate. They know the value
of getting things done now and eliminating the stress
that comes from unfinished business.

To overcome procrastination they:

- Break the task into manageable pieces
- Reward themselves for completing part of the
  task
- Develop a sense of urgency
- Affirm "Do it now, do it now, do it now!" over
  and over again

"Success is not forever and failure isn't fatal."

— Don Shula

51

TRASH

Even though Tod is a customer, we have been playing golf together a long time. We enjoy the game and the company - I give him 6 strokes a side and that gets us even up. We have developed games within the game to spice up every hole.

We play fairways, greens, sandies, birdies, polies (making a putt longer than the flagstick is high), and snakes (3 putts). Each piece of that trash is worth $.50 in addition to the hole. This helps us keep focused on all of the elements of the game and we are rewarded for doing the right things right and we have to pay for our mistakes.

Right now, I am $1.50 down on the trash. A lot more conversation takes place than money exchanged. It's pride that is at stake.

LEADERSHIP LESSONS FROM TRASH:

What you reward gets done. Successful leaders have a recognition and feedback system that rewards what needs to be done and does not reward activities they do not want to happen.

One of the basic communication needs from all employees is to know, "Does anyone care?" The reward system you put in place answers that question -- one way or another.

Successful leaders are creative in their approach to improvement. They know that you need small incentives to help you concentrate on your overall goals.

"The first essential, of course, is to know what you want."
— *Robert Collier*

6 FOOTER TO HALVE

The last hole is the signature hole. A 360 yard par four sounds simple but there is trouble everywhere. I am enjoying a career birdie day with 4. I also have 7 pars, 3 bogeys, 2 doubles and a quad. 6 over - not bad.

Tod is playing well also. He is seven over this side, thirteen over for the day. His four doubles have hurt. We are even in the round coming to the last hole, and he gets a stroke. We both play the hole well. I am six feet away from my par to halve the hole and split the match. Tod is in the hole with a bogey and hoping I will choke.

Six feet, just two paces - I have got to make this putt to halve the hole, split the match, and save my pride. Right now, I am the one feeling the pressure. I know what I have to do: six inch break left to right. Focus on the line, putter straight back, follow through, in the right lip -- no problem. It drops. Dead even match.

I shot a 78, Tod shot a 86 and we both walk away feeling like winners.

LEADERSHIP LESSONS FROM 6 FOOTER TO HALVE:

An outstanding leader keeps his cool under pressure. Worry drains your emotions and your strength. The effective leader focuses on the situation and takes action as opposed to being paralyzed by fear. You can eliminate worry by:

- Living one day at a time
- Dealing with the facts -- not perceptions
- Understand what is the worst possible outcome
- Begin immediately to improve upon the worst possible outcome

It is hard to worry about something you are working to take care of.

Successful leaders play with class -- win, lose, or draw. They make no excuses and look forward to the next challenge.

"Confidence doesn't come out of nowhere. It is a result of something...hours and days and weeks and years of constant work and dedication."

— *Roger Staubach*

LEADERSHIP MULLIGAN

*3 Keys to Managing Executive Stress:**
1. *Surround yourself with positive employees*
2. *Embrace change*
3. *Become resilient in attitude and action*

* *EPC International, Houston, TX*
Strategic Stress Consultants

HEAD TO HEAD

Tod has to go home early to watch his son's soccer match. Our business is settled, we split the match and I lose $1.50 on the trash. Tony still feels bad about the misclub. I gave him an extra $20 to take his wife out and forget about it. All in all, I played about as well as I can play.

The club's match play championship is next week. Three days of intense match play. Head to head, one on one, mono on mono -- that is the competition I enjoy. I get to see every one of my competitor's shots, get to play with his mind, and beat him about 6 and 5. I am excited about this tournament. I am going to the putting green and range to start getting ready.

LEADERSHIP LESSONS FROM HEAD TO HEAD:

Effective leaders are competitive and like to win straight up. The keys to maintaining your competitive edge are:

- Know what your competition is doing. Keep an eye on them and measure their successes and failures
- Enjoy the competition - it helps you get better
- Take no prisoners

Effective leaders have the self discipline to keep working long after their competitors have gone for the day.

The stamina to keep grinding when you are ready to give it up separates the winners from second place.

○ **Leaders know the difference in playing to win and playing not to lose.** That is the difference between their success and mediocrity.

○ **Leaders look to the future with optimism.** Regardless of the past, your future will be shaped by your optimism of what is ahead.

"Things turn out best for the people who make the best of the way things turn out.

– John Wooden

LINING UP
THE LOGO

I noticed today that Tod lined up his putts with the logo on his ball. This helped him keep the line and concentrate on hitting his putt solidly. I am going to try that on the putting green.

My last lesson from the pro was on keeping my left arm straight and following through. It sure helped me keep it in the fairway today.

The three things I am going to work on this practice are lining up my putts, keeping my left arm straight and my follow through.

Leadership Lessons From Lining Up The Logo:

Successful leaders never stop learning. Leaders learn from:

- Mentors who can relate their experiences
- Seminars or courses
- Reading something positive daily on how to improve their personal or professional life
- Associating with positive, successful people

Leaders keep improving even when they are at the top of their game. The best time to make personal and professional improvements is when things are going well. Your thought process is better, your stress level is less and your decisions are at their best.

"You can't ride on tracks you haven't laid down."
— Stan Davis, 2020 Vision

My Turn To Teach

Michael, my 10 year old son, is waiting for me at the range. I am teaching him some of the fundamentals I learned many years ago at the golf course. I think I can make a difference for him by sharing my experiences and teaching him what I know.

What I really enjoy is watching him grow, learning, and experimenting. I know he has many birdies, pars and bogies ahead.

After a great day, Michael and I head home. I agree with him when he says we need to come back tomorrow.

What a great game!

LEADERSHIP LESSONS FROM MY TURN TO TEACH:

Successful leaders are excellent teachers and develop their people. The keys to developing your people are:

- Provide them with opportunities for important and worthwhile contributions
- Encourage at every opportunity
- Show them how to develop and let them learn from your experience
- Develop yourself. Keep learning so you have more to teach

Leaders know that growing and developing their people is the true test of their leadership. Outstanding leaders help their followers become the leaders of the future.

"It is more blessed to give than to receive."

— *Acts 20:35*

APPENDIX

44 Leadership Lessons From the Links

1. Use technology to improve your effectiveness

2. *Hire the best people*

3. Dehire the people not right for the job

4. *Mentally prepare for the task at hand*

5. Have a guiding vision

6. *Have a plan to make your vision happen*

7. Create a positive environment while keeping a positive attitude

8. *Learn how to enjoy the good times while preparing for the challenging times*

9. Cope with the unexpected and create positive change

10. *Be a long term thinker*

11. Keep focused and concentrate on the critical success factors

44 LEADERSHIP LESSONS
FROM THE LINKS (CONTINUED)

12. *Recognize that the 80/20 rule applies in improving your organization*

13. Listen to your employees and act on their suggestions

14. *Make your meetings productive*

15. Set priorities

16. *Honor your employee's and customer's time*

17. Never sacrifice your integrity.

18. *Recognize that only integrity keeps followers*

19. Understand that your followers demand honesty

20. *Have a passion for leading*

21. Know that people only follow those that have a desire to lead

22. *Know how to solve problems quickly and efficiently.*

44 LEADERSHIP LESSONS
FROM THE LINKS (CONTINUED)

23. Recognize problems before they become an emergency

24. *Communicate with crystal clear clarity*

25. Accept responsibility

26. *Respect your employees before asking for their respect*

27. Have courage to take risks

28. *Look beyond the obstacles to the goal*

29. Utilize the capabilities of yourself and your people

30. *Work in your areas of excellence*

31. Don't live in past success, look for future success.

32. *Don't procrastinate, do it now!*

33. What you reward gets done

44 LEADERSHIP LESSONS
FROM THE LINKS (CONTINUED)

34. *Be creative in your approach to improvement*

35. Keep cool under pressure

36. *Play with class -- win, lose, or draw*

37. Be competitive

38. *Have the self discipline to keep working after others are gone*

39. Know the difference in playing to win and playing not to lose

40. *Look to the future with optimism*

41. Continue to learn from your people and external sources

42. *Keep improving even when you are at the top of your game*

43. Teach others

44. *Develop your people*

SCORECARD

HOLE	1	2	3	4	5	6	7	8	9	OUT	10	11	12	13	14	15	16	17	18	IN	TOTAL
PAR	4	4	4	5	3	5	3	4	4	36	4	4	3	4	5	3	4	5	4	36	72
YARDS	370	410	360	510	170	506	200	370	428	3324	425	414	160	396	496	150	402	545	360	3348	6672
HANDICAP	4	16	10	6	14	8	17	12	2		3	9	13	7	5	18	15	1	11		
DC	4	5	4	6	(2)	(4)	3	4	8	40	4	6	4	4	(4)	4	4	(4)	4	38	78
(10)	5	4	6	5	3	6	3	6	4	42	4	6	3	4	7	4	5	6	5	44	86
	\	-1	\	-1	\	+1		+2	+1		\	-1	-2	-3	-2		-1	\	\		

ACKNOWLEDGMENTS

I love golf and I love to teach leadership. The chance to put them together has been fun and exciting. My thanks to my family -- Karen, Jennifer, Kimberly, and Michael -- for helping me with the book and supporting me at home and at work.

Thanks to my golfing buddies that have provided me with these experiences -- Tod, Tony, Joe, Grady, Ken, Mark, Ty -- all have contributed to this book without knowing it. And my dad, Ralph Cottrell, who took the time to teach me the great game.

And finally to my assistant, Sherri Durham, who has kept the faith through all the years.

I hope you enjoyed the round.

About The Author

David Cottrell is President and CEO of CornerStone Leadership Institute. CornerStone teaches managers the concepts of leadership and is headquartered in Dallas, Texas.

A nationally known public speaker and business leadership consultant, he has trained over 11,000 managers at major corporations and has been a featured expert on public television.

Prior to CornerStone, Mr. Cottrell was a Senior Manager at Xerox and Federal Express. He also led the turnaround of a chapter eleven apparel company.

Mr. Cottrell is an avid golfer and carries a 6 handicap.

CornerStone Leadership Institute Offerings

- **Management Development Seminars**

    - *Building Your Leadership Foundation* - 1 Day Leadership Seminar designed to provide leaders and pre-leaders the necessary tools for their success
    - *The Foundation Program* - Leadership skill development workshop on the customer's site to reinforce the "7 Critical Skills for Leadership Success"

- **Management Retreat Speeches**

    - *Leadership Lessons On The Links.* A 30 to 45 minute light presentation that focuses on how lessons on the golf course can be applied in your business.

CornerStone Leadership Institute Offerings (continued)

- *What's Happened To Leadership?* A 20 to 30 minute presentation on leadership in the 90's

- **Customer Golf Outings or Sales Meetings** – Leadership Lessons on the Links presentation incorporating your company's goals and mission in a easily understood presentation.

- **In House Management Consulting** - Customized programs to address your areas of need in leadership and stress management.

CALL 1-888-789-LEAD
For Additional Information

CornerStone's
8 Keys to
Personal Security

1. Enjoy the victories

2. Keep your sense of humor

3. Master change

4. Keep your faith

5. Cultivate your family relationships

6. Have integrity

7. Develop your people

8. Get better every day